Writing

KATE CATON

TEACHER TIMESAVERS

Published by Scholastic Publications Ltd,
Villiers House,
Clarendon Avenue,
Leamington Spa,
Warwickshire CV32 5PR

© **1992 Scholastic Publications Ltd**

Author Kate Caton
Editor Margot O'Keeffe
Sub-editor Jo Saxelby
Series designer Joy White
Designers Anna Oliwa, Joy White
Illustrations Bernie Williams (Artquirks),
Lesley Smith (John Martin & Artists)
Cover illustration Frances Lloyd
Cover photograph Martyn Chillmaid

Designed using Aldus Pagemaker
Processed by Pages Bureau, Leamington Spa
Artwork by David Harban Design, Warwick
Printed and bound by Richard Clay Ltd, Bungay, Suffolk
NR35 1ED.

British Library Cataloguing-in-Publication Data
A catalogue record for this book is
available from the British Library.

ISBN 0-590-76405-5

Contents

This book contains 134 photocopiable sheets designed to help teachers implement the requirements for writing in the National Curriculum for English. The sheets are divided into eight topic areas and one General section which includes templates. The topic areas, which have been chosen because of their popularity in primary schools, are: Me and my family; Our school; Transport; Weather; Living things; Water; Food; Health and safety. The types of writing covered are shown on page 10.

The sheets can be used either as part of the work on an appropriate class topic or when a particular writing skill is the focus of a work session, for example letter or list writing. The use of some of the sheets may be prompted by circumstances at the time. For example, a foggy day may give rise to discussion and the story start sheet on page 62 could be used.

The sheets are suitable for use with individual children or groups. Within each topic area they are arranged in order according to the increasing level of ability required to complete them. Some of the more complex sheets may be simplified if required.

All the sheets will prompt discussion, either before the activity is worked on as part of the introduction or on completion. This discussion is as important as the recorded activity.

Encourage children to evaluate their own writing and to self-correct. Many of the sheets can be used for drafting. The photocopiable format allows teachers to give more than one copy of a sheet to each child for this purpose.

A sense of audience is important to good writing. Although not all writing needs to be prepared for formal display, children will enjoy sharing their work with others. These sheets are an ideal way of building up class scrapbooks or individual books/folders for that purpose.

Some activities, such as story starts and letter writing, are common to each topic section. General information on using these sheets is given below and therefore the specific teachers' notes refer you back to this page.

Picture story starters
At the beginning of each topic section, there is a sheet which offers the youngest children a visual prompt to writing which may be imaginative or descriptive. Read the initial instruction to the children and help them match the words to the picture. Less able children could use a tape recorder to talk about the picture.

Story starts
These sheets provide the beginning of a story which the children then complete themselves. Read the story start through with the children and let them offer various suggestions as to how the story may continue and end. Then let them write on their own, encouraging them to use their imaginations.

Story middles and ends
In each topic section the story middles and ends are presented on the same sheet and should be cut apart once photocopied. It is intended that children use these sheets as prompts for stories which they can write on a separate sheet of paper. Discussion on the importance of clear story structure, for example a beginning, middle and end, should precede the writing activity.

Story strip sheets
In several of the sections there are activities which require the children to use the blank story strip sheet on page 131 in the General section.

Encourage clear progression in the story-telling and small, neat handwriting.

Letter-writing activities
Some of the topic sections include ideas for children's letter writing. Following each of these is a sheet of illustrated notepaper which should be photocopied and placed over a copy of the letter template on page 132 in the General section. This template will encourage children to set out their letters in the correct format. The children can make an envelope for their letters using the template on page 133 in the General section.

World of work sheets
Some of the sections feature an activity that requires the use of the World of work sheet which is in the General section on page 134. This sheet provides a ready format for the children to set out the information on jobs they have researched. The box in the right-hand corner is for a picture, which could be hand-drawn or cut out from a magazine. Children can fill in the section at the bottom ('A working day in the life of..') in whatever style they wish, for example prose, diary, notes and so on.

Me and my family

In the garden See note above on picture story starters.
Find the word This is a labelling activity. Talk about the picture with the children. Help them to read the instructions and words. Explain how to label the items and that small, neat handwriting will be required.

Parts of the body Help the children to identify the parts of the body indicated and to read the words given. The children could add other parts of the body not listed here.

We like... Talk about the names of the people and the activities shown. Explain how the mapping activity is carried out and discuss with the children what their sentences are likely to say. Different combinations are possible, for example, Dad may like to read or fish. Encourage correct use of capital letters and full stops.

What did they say? Writing in speech bubbles does not require speech mark punctuation and is therefore a good way of introducing the concept of speech in writing.

My (sister)... The main title and four sub-titles can be changed to suit different family members. Using 'my sister' as an example, talk about the likely words and phrases that will be used. The children can draw a portrait of their family member in the frame provided.

Story start See note on story start sheets on page 5.

My day/A letter to... This sheet comprises two separate activities and should be cut in half when photocopied. For 'My day', see note on story strip sheets on page 5. For 'A letter to...', see note on letter-writing activities on page 5.

Letter-writing paper To be used with the previous activity. See page 5.

All about ME! This sheet requires the children to write down information about themselves and can be an introduction to form-filling. Some children will need help to find out some information, for example their address, height and weight. Ask the children who might want to know the information they have written.

Story middle/Story end See note on story middles and ends on page 5.

My friend This sheet asks the children to think in some detail about a friend and to write about him or her. Read the instructions and questions with the children. A picture of the friend can be drawn and coloured in the space provided.

Let's write a poem Read the poem with the children. Talk about the rhythm and rhymes. Let the children suggest about whom they would like to write a poem. Stress that the poems do not have to rhyme.

Family tree Discuss the relationships shown on the family tree. When the children have understood the concept, read through the instructions with them and let them answer the questions given. Remember to be sensitive to children not in a 'normal' family situation.

Ben's family This sheet looks at different members of a family and what they are called. If necessary, help the children at first and then let them continue on their own. The word 'grandmother' runs downwards.

Our school

Time for school See note on picture story starters on page 5.

Accident! Discuss with the children what is happening in the pictures and what the possible outcomes could be. They should draw the outcome they decide on in the blank box, then write the story. It may be helpful to display a list of useful words. Younger or less able children could tell the story using a tape recorder.

Classroom crossword Some children may need help with spelling. The answers are: 1 table; 2 chair; 3 Lego; 4 gerbil; 5 book; 6 pencil; 7 crayon; 8 brush; 9 teacher; 10 paint.

My teacher... Read the 'titles' of the four sections and discuss the sorts of words, phrases or sentences that may be written in each one.

My best day at school/Jobs in school This sheet comprises two separate activities and should be cut in half when photocopied. For 'My best day at school', see note on using the story strip sheet on page 5. For 'Jobs in school', see note on using the World of Work sheet on page 5.

My school friend Discuss the information that will give a good description of a friend. Encourage capital letters and full stops.

School work Talk about the pictures which represent the different areas of the curriculum. Ask the children to suggest names for some of the areas before they work on the sheet. The word 'caretaker' runs downwards.

School rules Discuss with the children what rules are and why they are needed. Read through the sheet with the children and discuss any new rules they might add. Is it possible to implement any of them?

What are they saying? Look at each picture together and read the question underneath. Let the children suggest what dialogue might be spoken. One example is done for them. Discuss the use of speech/quotation marks.

Story start See note on story start sheets on page 5.

Story middle/Story end See note on story middles and ends on page 5.

My favourite subjects The results of this activity may be quite enlightening and provide an insight into a child's real interests. The activity will help to develop list writing and descriptive writing.

Job swap Emphasise the need for sentences demarcated with capital letters and full stops.

A way to school This sheet could be used with pages 119 and 129 as part of a road safety topic. Discuss with the children the various routes Tommy might take to school and the hazards which must be avoided. This activity will encourage directional skills and could be extended to work on the children's own journey to school.

School pets If there are no school pets children could write about what pets they might like.

Transport

In the town See note on picture story starters on page 5.

Off we go on the train Talk through the sheet with the children, looking at each picture and reading the words. The children need to fill in the missing words. They can then draw their picture of a train and write about it.

Wordsearch Some children will be familiar with the wordsearch procedure but this needs to be confirmed. All the words read across.

Ways of travelling The given sentence can be used as a model for sentences based on colour - or you could encourage the children to be more imaginative. It may be useful to display a list of the different types of transport to help with spelling problems.

Find the word The word 'transport' can be found reading downwards.

Rhyming words The sheet might be introduced by brainstorming rhyming words for the first picture. Discuss the fact that rhyming words may not always have the same spelling pattern - such as train, lane. Let the children share their sentences which are bound to be nonsensical and amusing.

Where are the words? Some of the words in this wordsearch read downwards.

Story start See note on story start sheets on page 5.

Story middle/Story end See note on story middles and ends on page 5.

Air travel, Water travel, Land travel Each of these sheets requires the children to make a list and then to produce a piece of factual writing. They will need relevant books to carry out the research for their work.

Off to work/Time for a story This sheet comprises two separate activities and should be cut in half when photocopied. For 'Off to work', see note on using the World of work sheet on page 5. For 'Time for a story', see note on using the story strip sheet on page 5.

Find me! The words read diagonally, across and downwards. Ask the children to invent a way of timing themselves which does not involve using a watch or clock? The 12 words to be found are: hydrofoil; helicopter; tandem; surfboard; tricycle; hovercraft; ferry; glider; bicycle; canoe; truck; coach.

Give us a clue! This crossword needs nine more clues. They must be very short - about six to eight words. Encourage the children to be as concise as possible, and to try their puzzles out on a friend or family member.

Weather

Sun time See note on picture story starters on page 5.

Heat wave The children should write words or phrases that say how they feel, what they like doing and what they wear when it is very hot. The outcome could be used as the basis for extended prose or poetry writing.

What is the weather like? Let the children read the words and talk about the pictures. Read the instructions together and perhaps do the first picture orally before they complete the sheet on their own.

How do they feel? This sheet explores feelings. The children interpret a situation and describe what the people illustrated might be feeling. Discuss any similar situations in which the children have been involved.

Holiday postcard Discuss the sort of things people write about on postcards, such as the weather, their activities, where they are staying. Emphasise that small, neat writing is necessary, that the address should be correctly laid out and that the message should be short and lively.

The weather is... Read through the instructions with the children and talk about the pictures before they work on this sheet. The answers are: windy; freezing; hailing; misty; hot; wet; raining. The word 'weather' can be found reading downwards.

Story start See note on story start sheets on page 5.

Story middle/Story end See note on story middles and ends on page 5.

Faulty forecast/TV weather person This sheet comprises two separate activities and should be cut in half when photocopied. For 'Faulty forecast', see note on letter-writing activities on page 5. For 'Television weather person', see note on the World of work sheet on page 5. This sheet could be a follow-up activity to 'Faulty forecast'.

Letter-writing paper To be used with 'Faulty forecast'. See page 5.

My weather diary Choose a good place to place a thermometer in order to record the temperature twice daily. Encourage the children to use words that really describe what the weather is like, for example chilly or humid.

Bad weather! The children are asked to write poems with each line starting with a particular letter, acrostic-style. Discuss the subject of each poem and let the children suggest appropriate words and phrases.

Drought This sheet provides an opportunity for evaluative writing based on previous knowledge or research. The word clues can be used as prompts for discussion or research.

Snow Read the descriptive passage with the children and discuss the use of adjectives to 'paint a mental picture'.

Newsworthy This sheet can be used by individual children or groups. Discuss what events might be newsworthy and, specifically, about what is happening in the picture. Read some newspaper articles to familiarise the children with the tone and style in which these are written. Talk about headlines and picture captions that are eye-catching and have an instant impact on the reader.

Living things

Animal farm See note on picture story starters on page 5.

How do they move? The children are asked to classify creatures according to the way they move. Either discuss the various modes of animal movement with the children first or help them to research the information. Some animals may fit into more than one category.

Caring for a pet/A puppy is for life! This sheet comprises two separate activities and should be cut in half when photocopied. For 'Caring for a pet', see note on the story strip sheet on page 5. This sheet requires sequenced instruction writing. Discuss the important points of pet care that the children need to illustrate and write about. For 'A puppy is for life!', see note on letter-writing activities on page 5.

Letter-writing paper To be used with 'A puppy is for life!'. See page 5.

Mr Pricklepin, Freddie the fish, Leo the lion These open-ended sheets can be used in a number of ways to stimulate both factual and creative writing. The spaces in the animal outlines can be filled in with appropriate vocabulary by teacher or pupil, and used as the basis for the writing. For example, children might describe the appearance and behaviour of the creature or write a short story or riddle.

Read all about it The children are asked to write an article for a given headline - see the notes for page 70 'Newsworthy'.

Where is it? Work on compass points is necessary before handing out this sheet.

Story start See note on story start sheets on page 5.

Story middle/Story end See note on story middles and ends on page 5.

Safari park poster Read the instructions with the children and discuss their ideas for making the poster easy to read and eye-catching.

Let's talk! The children may like to make the puppets before or after writing the conversation. They will need to name the characters that speak. A discussion about use of speech marks and/or drama format would be useful.

My farm-i-o! Talk about the pattern of the chorus and verse and let the children identify the rhyming words.

My Spidergram The children will need to carry out some research on spiders before they can write in the facts.

Water

Let's go for a swim See note on picture story starters on page 5.

Waterfall crossword Look through the sheet together and let the children talk about the illustrations before they do the crossword.

Label it Read through the words to make sure the children are familiar with them.

Wet! Wet! Wet! The children can use the words given on the sheet to help with their captions. This sheet provides an opportunity to talk about verbs.

Finish and join Some children may need help to complete the words in this activity before joining the object with its name.

At the seaside Talk with the children about what they can see, smell, feel and like doing at the seaside. Their suggestions can be written in the seaside shapes as words or phrases. The completed sheet could then be used as the basis for extended writing.

All jumbled up! This sequencing exercise can either be completed in the way suggested on the sheet or the children can cut out each sentence to place them in order before writing the correct order on the sheet.

It sounds like rain! This sheet gives an onomatopoeic poem as an example for the children to follow. Talk about other 'watery words' that they can use in their poems.

Frogs Look together at books about frogs. On the sheet, pictures are given to show the life-cycle of the frog. The children are asked to write a sentence for each picture. Emphasise that small, neat and concise writing is required.

Fresh water or salt water This sheet asks the children to find out about freshwater and salt-water creatures. It provides a categorising activity and a factual writing exercise.

Story start See note on story start sheets on page 5.

Story middle/Story end See note on story middles and ends on page 5.

The crazy boat race The children are asked to write a newspaper article. While they should be creative in their writing, remind them about journalistic style.

The water cycle/The life-guard This sheet comprises two separate activities and should be cut in half when photocopied. For 'The water cycle', see note on story strip sheet on page 5. For 'The life-guard', see note on letter-writing activities on page 5.

Letter-writing paper To be used with 'The life-guard'. See page 5.

Food

It's party time! See note on picture story starters on page 5.

Choose the colour Discuss food colours with the children. Encourage them to use capital letters and full stops when writing sentences.

What should we eat? Discuss the necessity of food and the different sorts of foods, such as vegetables, meats, fish and fruit. Look at the sheet with the children. The sheet involves evaluative list writing.

The food factory This sheet focuses on the senses and requires the children to use their imagination. Let them talk about the illustration before they write about it. Encourage them to make verbal suggestions about what they might see, smell, hear and taste in the factory.

What happened? The children are asked to describe the events in the pictures. In the last picture space they must draw the end of the story and write a description of it alongside. Encourage creativity in devising unusual outcomes.

Healthy eating The hidden word in the puzzle is 'delicious'.

Let's go shopping This sheet provides a good opportunity to check the children's knowledge of alphabetical order.

Story start See note on story start sheets on page 5.

Story middle/Story end See note on story middles and ends on page 5.

Who's cooking?/Invent a lolly This sheet comprises two separate activities and should be cut in half when photocopied. For 'Who's cooking?', see note on the World of work sheet on page 5. For 'Invent a lolly', see note on letter-writing activities on page 5.

Letter-writing paper To be used with 'Invent a lolly'. See page 5.

Let's have a party Invitation writing requires concise information. Let the children discuss their ideas and suggestions before beginning their first draft.

Let's have a barbecue The children are asked to choose a menu for a barbecue. Let them suggest which foods they would like to eat, and encourage them to suggest foods which contribute to a healthy, well-balanced diet.

The sandwich bar Discuss with the children the different steps involved in making a sandwich. Talk about the need for the instructions to be concise. Healthy eating and hygiene are important considerations.

Tasty crossword Children are asked to write the clues for a completed crossword. Encourage them to try out their clues on a friend - they will need to draw an empty crossword grid on another sheet.

Health and safety

Fire! Fire! See note on picture story starters on page 5.

Dental wordsearch It may be a good idea to find together one of the words that reads downwards. Then let the children complete the sheet on their own or in pairs.

Spot the hazards! Children are asked to draw a ring round each hazard. Younger children could perhaps write one word about each hazard. More able or older children can write a phrase or sentence about each. Useful discussion on safety could follow this activity.

Out and about/This is my job This sheet comprises two separate activities and should be cut in half when photocopied. For 'Out and about', see note on the story strip sheet on page 5. For 'This is my job', see note on the World of work sheet on page 5.

Beware! Make sure that all the children are familiar with the wordsearch procedure. Discuss what link each word has with danger.

Healthy food This sheet concerns balanced diet and could be used in conjunction with pages 112 and 113 in the 'Food' section. Children are required to extract information from a diagram and then select relevant parts of it for their own purpose - in this case, menu writing.

Taking exercise! This sheet emphasises the importance of exercise. The children write a list, and produce a piece of free writing.

Story start See note on story start sheets on page 5.

Story middle/Story end See note on story middles and ends on page 5.

Competition time! Talk about what makes a good poster. Is it eye-catching? Is it clear? Can you read it from a distance? Does it contain all the information? Discuss the styles and sizes of handwriting to be used. The posters could be judged by the children themselves, or invitations extended to judges selected by the children.

Toothy tales This question and answer sheet emphasises the importance of cleaning teeth. Encourage complete sentences with capital letters and full stops. Mirrors may be needed, or the children can help one another by counting each other's teeth.

Water safety Discuss the dangers of water play with the children and how these dangers can be avoided. Younger children can write short descriptive phrases to go with the pictures, while older or more able children can write imperative sentences appropriate to rules.

Safety rhymes Talk about how 'I hear thunder' (or Frère Jacques) has been used as a pattern for this new rhyme. Ask the children to suggest other possible 'pattern' rhymes, before they draft their own road safety rhymes.

On the road Copies of 'The Highway Code' would be useful for this activity, which will be particularly relevant to children taking a cycling proficiency course. Ask them which signs in their locality give information to the public.

Keep fit! Discuss different strategies for finding the words, for example scanning for initial letters. The 12 words are: toothbrush; dentist; exercise; vegetables; doctor; warmth; nurse; nourishment; water; sleep; vitamins; cleanliness.

General section

Story strip sheet, Letter template, Envelope template, World of work sheet See notes on page 5.

Book review sheet It is a useful exercise for children to report on a book they have read. It provides opportunity for summative and evaluative writing. These sheets could be made available all the time so that the children can report on something they have read while it is fresh in their minds.

My diary This sheet can be used throughout the year to record the events of each day, to review the past week or for a holiday diary. Children might write in note form or continuous prose - both of which might be used at a later time as the basis for extended writing.

The great debate Explain to the children the concept of a reasoned argument and the possibility of opposing opinions. The children will use this sheet to list the arguments for and against the chosen issue, to formulate an opinion and might go on to write an appropriate speech, perhaps for a proper class debate. The issue can be chosen by the teacher or the children.

Book jacket This sheet is an aid to presenting the children's writing. Enlarge on the photocopier as necessary. Discuss with the children the information a book jacket carries and why.

Sell it! Draw or stick a black and white magazine cut-out picture of a suitable product on a first photocopy of this sheet. Now use this as the master sheet to copy. Discuss with the children the characteristics of persuasive advertising slogans and jingles - eg they are short, memorable and emphasise the features of the product which make it more outstanding than its competitors.

Punctuation This sheet comprises three separate passages for punctuating. They increase in difficulty from top to bottom. The passages should be cut out and used individually.

Alphabet Arthur This dot-to-dot activity requires the children to use their knowledge of the alphabet. It can be used as a starting point for more alphabetical work. The children are also asked to write about the picture they create.

What's the message? Taking a message in note form is an important skill. This exercise will show the children the importance of recording the main points of a message.

Crack the code! Both encoding and decoding skills are required. Make sure all the children understand how the different letters are found.

Picture puzzle This is a rebus 'puzzle letter'. The children have to work out what the note says and are encouraged to do some 'picture writing' of their own.

Below is a grid showing the types of writing covered in this book.

Descriptive prose	11, 22, 26, 31, 37, 40, 41, 56, 57, 59, 69, 71, 75, 76, 77, 86, 91, 101, 104, 116
Diary	66, 136
Evaluative	68, 103, 135, 137
Graphical	
Information	24, 72, 79, 121, 129
Informational	
Prose	30, 50, 51, 52, 53, 64, 68, 75, 76, 77, 85, 94, 95, 99, 110, 118, 119, 122, 134
Instructions/rules	33, 39, 73, 114, 119, 127
Labels/captions	12, 13, 70, 78, 88, 89, 98
Letter	18, 19, 60, 64, 65, 73, 74, 99, 100, 110, 111, 112, 132, 133
List	33, 37, 50, 51, 52, 103, 107, 122
Newspaper	70, 78, 98
Note	20, 31, 134, 142
Personal	16, 20, 38
Poetry/Rhyme	23, 46, 67, 84, 93, 128, 139
Poster	82, 113, 125, 138
Puzzle	25, 28, 32, 43, 45, 47, 54, 55, 61, 87, 90, 106, 115, 117, 120, 130, 141, 143, 144
Sentence	14, 29, 42, 44, 58, 92, 102, 126, 140
Speech	15, 34, 83
Story	17, 21, 27, 35, 36, 48, 49, 62, 63, 80, 81, 96, 97, 105, 108, 109, 123, 124
Story strip	18, 30, 53, 73, 99, 119, 131

Name _____

In the garden

What is happening in the picture?

♣ Write about the picture.
Here are some words to help you:

Gran	washing
Dad	flowers
Mum	digging
baby	swing
boy	playhouse
girl	motor bike
reading	

♣ Think of a title for your writing.

_____

_____

_____

_____

_____

Find the word

Find the word

✤ Write these words in the right spaces on the picture.

| chair | cat | tap | door | table | dog | baby | window |

✤ Write a sentence about the picture. _____

_____

✤ Think of a good title for the picture. _____

Parts of the body

♣ How many parts of the body can you name? The words below will help you.

♣ Write the name for each part in the right space.

♣ Think of three more parts of the body. Write them alongside the right part of the picture.

knee	chest
leg	head
eye	foot
arm	hand
mouth	nose

Me and my family

We like...

Name _____

We like...

Who likes to do **what**? →

Gran → garden

1 <u>Mum likes to garden._____</u>

Mum read

2 _____

Dad swim

3 _____

Pat skip

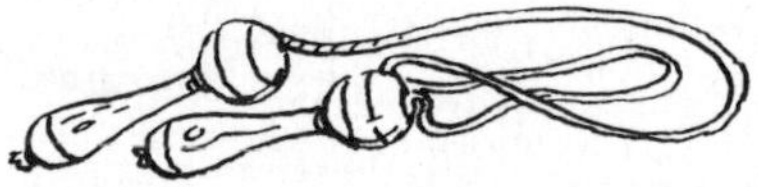

4 _____

Sam fish

5 _____

Jill play football

6 _____

♣ What do you like to do? _____

Name _____

What did they say?

❖ Draw a picture of you doing something with someone in your family. What did you say?
Write it in a speech bubble.

My (sister)...

likes

doesn't like

My _____

plays

wears

Name _____

❖ Continue the story and give your story a title.

It was the day of my _____ th birthday and Mr Magic had come to my party to entertain us all. He had shown us several tricks when suddenly, something **really** magical happened!

Name _____

My day

♣ Think about the different things you do and the places you go to during your day.

♣ Using the story strip sheet, draw pictures and write captions to show the different parts of your day.

Will you include some of these activities?

- getting up
- going to school
- watching television
- having a swimming lesson
- playing with a friend
- going to bed

♣ What else will you include?

A letter to...

People love to receive letters.

♣ Write to someone who would like to hear about you and your family – perhaps a pen-pal or a neighbour who has moved away.

♣ Tell them what the family has been doing, where you have been, what visitors you have had, what happened at school and other interesting news.

♣ Use the letter template under your writing paper.

From our house...

To you

Name _____

All about ME!

♣ Fill in the form with information all about you. You may need to weigh and measure yourself and look in a mirror!

Name _____

Address _____

_____

_____ Post code _____

Date of birth _____

Age _____

Height _____

Weight _____

My hair colour is _____

My eyes are _____

I live with _____

My hobbies are _____

My school is _____

_____

This is ME!

Story middle

♣ Write a story with a beginning, a middle and an end. Use the sentences below as part of the **middle** of your story.

Suddenly there I was, hanging on as tightly as I could to stop myself from falling. Whatever could I do to save myself?

❗ Remember to give your story a title.

Story end

♣ Write a story with a beginning, a middle and an end. Use the sentences below as the **end** of your story.

We took the little old man into our house and sat him down in front of the fire. After a hot cup of tea and some of Mum's special crispy biscuits, we took him back to his home. It had been a very worrying, but exciting, afternoon.

❗ Remember to give your story a title.

My friend

Everyone has a friend they know very well.

❖ Write about your friend and then draw his or her picture.

- What does your friend look like?
- What does your friend like to do?
- Why do you like him or her?
- Where does your friend live?
- What do you like to do together?

_____

_____

_____

_____

_____

_____

Writing

Let's write a poem

This is a poem someone made up about their baby brother.

What my baby brother enjoys,
Is making lots and lots of noise.
He bangs his drum
Which makes me glum.
Why can't they buy him *quiet* toys?

♣ Write a poem about someone you live with.
You may decide to make some of the words rhyme.

♣ You could write more verses about other people you live with.

Name _____

Family tree

Family tree

A 'family tree' is a diagram that shows how a family is built up over several generations.
❧ Look at this family tree and then write sentences to answer the questions (ⓜ means 'married').

❧ Who did Cyril Smith marry?

❧ Who had three children?

❧ What are the names of Jane Smith's two grandmothers?

❧ What is the relationship between Lucy Smith and George Jones?

❧ How many nieces does Nancy Smith have? Who are they?

❧ Now you try and draw someone's family tree. It could be yours!

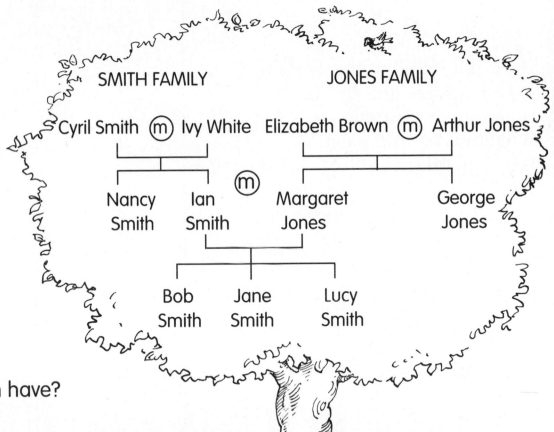

SMITH FAMILY   JONES FAMILY

Cyril Smith ⓜ Ivy White   Elizabeth Brown ⓜ Arthur Jones

Nancy Smith   Ian Smith   ⓜ   Margaret Jones   George Jones

Bob Smith   Jane Smith   Lucy Smith

Ben's family

Different members of a family are known by different names.

✤ Work out the names of Ben's family members in the list below.

- Ben's father's father is Ben's ___ ___ ___ ___ ___ ___ ___ ___ ___ ___ ___ ___

- Ben's parents' daughter is Ben's ___ ___ ___ ___ ___ ___

- Ben's male parent is his ___ ___ ___ ___ ___ ___

- Ben's aunt's child is Ben's ___ ___ ___ ___ ___

- Ben's sister is his parents' ___ ___ ___ ___ ___ ___ ___ ___

- Ben's female parent is his ___ ___ ___ ___ ___ ___

- Ben is his parents' ___ ___ ___

- Ben's father's sister is Ben's ___ ___ ___ ___

- The son of Ben's aunt is Ben's mother's ___ ___ ___ ___ ___

- The daughter of Ben's aunt is Ben's mother's ___ ___ ___ ___ ___

- Ben's parents' other son is Ben's ___ ___ ___ ___ ___ ___ ___

✤ Can you spot a hidden relation? Her name reads downwards.
She is Ben's ___ ___ ___ ___ ___ ___ ___ ___ ___ ___ ___

Name _____

Time for school

Time for school

What a busy classroom!

♣ Write about the picture.
Here are some words to help you:

painting   Lego
clay   computer
gerbils   game
weighing   teacher
writing   children
reading   sand

♣ Think of a title for your writing.

_____

_____

_____

_____

_____

Name _____

Accident!

♣ Draw what happened next.

♣ Tell the story.

_____

_____

_____

_____

_____

Name _____

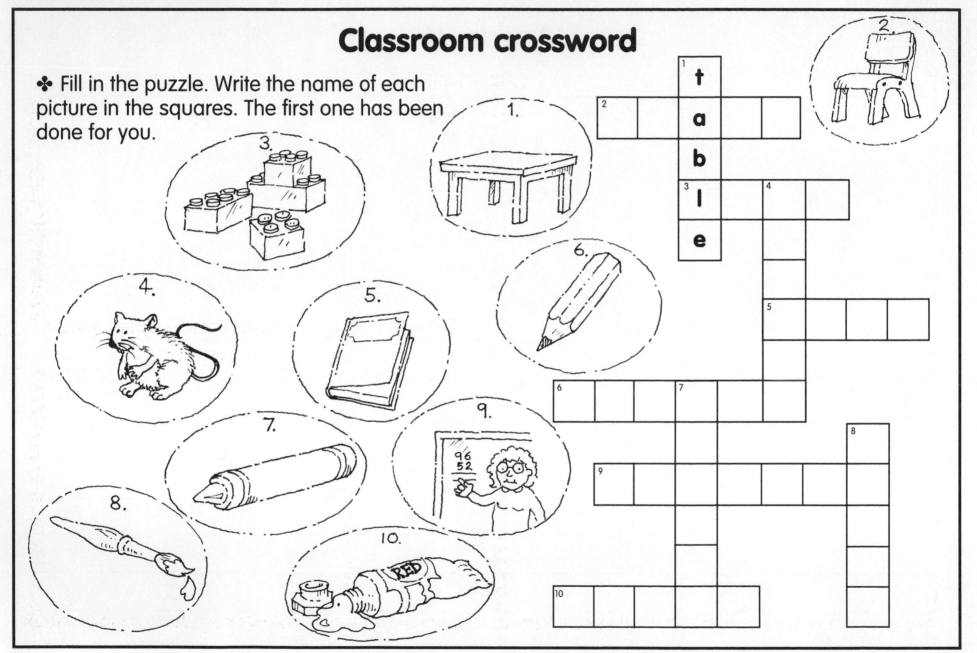

Classroom crossword

♣ Fill in the puzzle. Write the name of each picture in the squares. The first one has been done for you.

My teacher...

likes it when

gets cross when

wears

is good at

Name _____

My best day at school

♣ Think about your day in school. If you could change things, what would your day be like?

♣ Using the story strip sheet, draw pictures and write captions to show what you would like to happen during your best school day.

What different things would you do?

What would you wear?

What time would school start and end?

Jobs in school

Here is a list of some people who work in school:

headteacher
teacher
secretary
cook
caretaker
governor

You may think of others!

♣ Choose a job done by someone who works in your school. By talking to the person who does the job, find out as much as you can about it.

♣ Write about the job on your World of work sheet.

My school friend

♣ Choose a school friend to write about.
Ask your friend some questions.
Make your notes here.

Name _____ Age _____

Birthday _____

Hair colour _____ Height _____

Brothers/sisters _____

Favourite TV programme _____

_____

Hobbies _____

What do you like doing with your friend?

_____

What is special about your friend?

_____

♣ Draw a picture of your friend here.

♣ Use your notes to write a description of your friend here.

Name _____

School work

There are lots of things to learn about at school.

♣ See if you can work out what the different subjects are. There are some letters and pictures to help you.

♣ If you have filled in the puzzle correctly, you will find the hidden word. What is it?

(CLUE: He looks after the school and keeps it in good order.)

School rules

All schools have rules.
✤ Think of four rules that you have in your school. They might be classroom rules or playground rules.

✤ List them here.

✤ Choose a new rule that you think your school should have.

✤ Make a poster or notice telling everyone the new rule. Where would you put your notice?

What are they saying?

What are they saying?

♣ Write what they are saying. Remember to use speech marks.
One story is done for you.

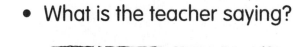

'This will be good and strong now, but no more swinging on the net,' he warned.

_____
_____
_____
_____
_____
_____

- What is the caretaker saying?

- What is the teacher saying?

_____
_____
_____
_____

_____
_____
_____
_____
_____

- What is the cook saying?

- What is the child saying?

2 + 4 =
5 + 3 =

34

❖ Continue the story and give your story a title.

Duncan shuffled into his classroom and sat down at his table with a thud. He was not looking forward to another boring day at school. Just then he noticed a message pinned on to the board.

Name _____

Story middle

♣ Write a story with a beginning, a middle and an end. Use the sentences below as part of the **middle** of your story.

We were right in the middle of the relay race when it happened. Roger was the second person in the Blue's relay team and as he turned to grab the baton from Kirsty

! Remember to give your story a title.

Story end

♣ Write a story with a beginning, a middle and an end. Use the sentences below as the **end** of your story.

The school fête had been brilliant! Liam had won a coconut, a bottle of pop and a huge cake. He had spent *all* his money but he didn't care. He'd had *such* a good time, and to think that it had all started so badly!

! Remember to give your story a title.

My favourite subjects

We learn about many different things at school.
♣ Make a list of all the different sorts of work you do, such as maths and science.

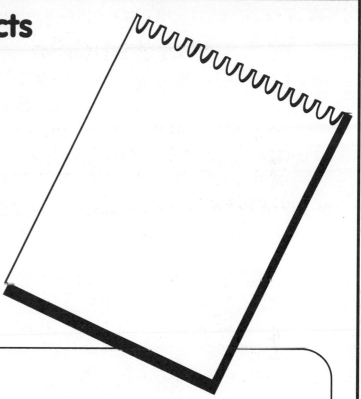

♣ Write the number 1 next to the type of work you like best. Then number the other activities in order from best to worst.

♣ Think about what you like to do best and write about it. Describe the sort of work you do and say why you like doing it.

Name _____

Job swap

If you could swap places with your headteacher, how would you spend your day?

♣ What jobs would you have to do?

♣ What changes would you like to make in your school?

♣ What would you like about the job?

♣ What would you dislike?

Name _____

A way to school

✤ Work out a safe route for Tommy to walk to school. (Draw it on to the map in pencil so that you can rub it out later.)

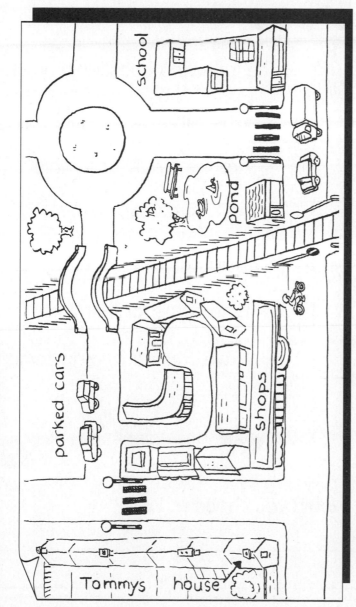

✤ Write out the instructions for your route here.

✤ Now rub out your pencil lines from the map.
✤ Give this sheet to a friend to see if she or he can follow your instructions.

Name _____

School pets

School pets

♣ What types of animals do you have in your school? Write about them.

The following questions may help you.

- What are the animals' names?

- Are they male or female?

- Where do they sleep?

- What do they eat and drink?

- Who cares for them?

- Have you learned anything from them?

♣ If you could have another pet at school, what would you choose? Why?

_____

_____

Writing

Name _____

In the town

The town is very busy.
How many different kinds of
transport can you see?

♣ Write about the picture.
Here are some words to help you:

car	bus
van	coach
bike	motor cycle
taxi	driver
people	traffic jam

♣ Think of a title for your writing.

_____

_____

_____

_____

_____

Name _____

Off we go on the train

Off we go on the train

✤ Fill in the words to finish the sentences.

Here is the _____

We get _____ the _____

We show our_____

Here is the _____

We get _____ the _____

✤ Draw a train and write a sentence about it.

Writing

Name _____

Wordsearch

♣ Can you find the words below in the puzzle?
♣ Draw a ring round each one. One has been done for you.

| c a r | b u s | t r a i n | b i k e | b o a t | p l a n e | s h i p | l o r r y |

a	z	b	y	c	s	h	i	p	x	e
w	c	a	r	g	v	i	u	k	t	m
h	j	l	n	p	b	u	s	r	s	v
z	a	y	b	x	c	w	d	v	e	u
b	f	p	l	a	n	e	c	g	d	h
e	c	f	e	g	m	h	n	i	o	j
k	a	l	i	t	r	a	i	n	m	g
b	i	k	e	n	a	o	c	p	e	q
o	t	n	s	m	r	l	o	r	r	y
z	g	y	b	o	a	t	h	x	i	w
o	b	q	c	s	d	u	e	w	f	y

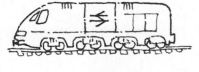

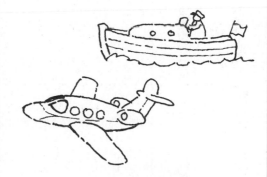

Ways of travelling

Ways of travelling

♣ Colour each type of transport a different colour.

♣ Write a sentence about each type of transport.
One has been done for you.

1 _The motor bike is black._

2 _____

3 _____

4 _____

5 _____

6 _____

Find the word

♣ Solve the puzzle and find the hidden word. Some letters have been put in to help you.

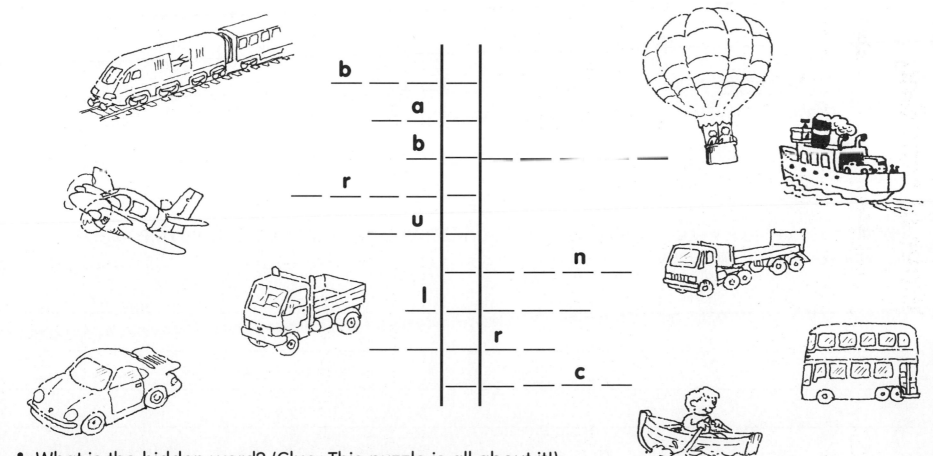

b ___ ___

___ a ___

___ b ___ ___ ___ ___ ___ ___ ___

___ r ___ ___

___ u ___

___ ___ n ___

___ l ___ ___

___ r ___ ___

___ c ___

♣ What is the hidden word? (Clue: This puzzle is all about it!)

Name _____

Rhyming words

♣ Think of at least five rhyming words for each picture.
♣ Write them next to the picture. Some have been done for you.

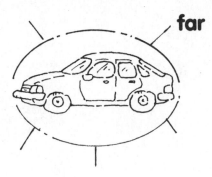 **far**

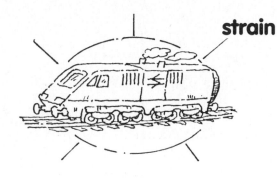 **strain**

sip

♣ Write a sentence for each picture using as many of your rhyming words as possible.
Will your sentences be funny?

_____

_____

_____

_____

Where are the words?

There are seven words hidden in the square – but where?
They may be written across or downwards.
♣ Draw a ring round each word you find. The pictures will help you.

a	m	b	l	c	k	d	j	t	i	e	g
c	l	o	r	r	y	e	d	a	f	h	f
g	b	h	x	i	a	j	z	x	y	k	v
r	l	c	p	s	m	t	n	l	u	w	o
o	q	o	m	p	n	q	l	r	k	s	j
h	t	a	u	g	f	e	r	r	y	i	t
g	f	c	e	v	d	w	c	x	b	y	a
l	a	h	z	x	q	y	r	z	s	a	n
i	p	v	o	u	n	t	m	l	z	y	d
d	w	t	r	i	c	y	c	l	e	k	e
e	f	g	t	u	h	v	i	w	j	x	m
r	s	e	r	d	q	c	p	b	o	a	n

Story start

Name _____

♣ Continue the story and give your story a title.

'I can't imagine anyone wanting this rickety old pram,' said Dad. 'I'll take it to the rubbish tip.' As he threw it into the van, the large wheels glinted in the sun.

'No, don't!' shouted David. 'I'm sure we could use those wheels.'

'Of course we could,' said Debbie. 'We could make a

Story middle

❖ Write a story with a beginning, a middle and an end. Use the sentences below as part of the **middle** of your story.

Danielle's Mum came round to the passenger's side of the car. 'Yes! You're absolutely right! We *have* got a puncture,' she said.

'Oh no!' whined Danielle. 'That means we're going to be late! We'll miss the start of the show! What shall we do?'

❗ Remember to give your story a title.

Story end

❖ Write a story with a beginning, a middle and an end. Use the sentences below as the **end** of your story.

Danny felt a slight bump and knew that his magic carpet had landed. As his eyes became used to the dark, he realised he was back in his own bedroom. What an adventure he had had! Was it all a dream?

❗ Remember to give your story a title.

Air travel

♣ How do we travel in the air?

♣ What do we travel in?

♣ How many different ways of travelling in the air can you think of?

♣ Make a list here.

♣ Choose one form of air travel and find out as much as you can about it. When was it invented? What is it made from? How does it move? What else can you find out?

♣ Write about it here.

Water travel

* How do we travel on the water?
* What do we travel on?
* How many ways of travelling on the water can you think of?
* Make a list here.

* Choose one form of water travel and find out as much as you can about it. When was it invented? How does it move? What is it made from? What else can you find out?
* Write about it here.

Writing

Name _____

Land travel

How do we travel across the land?

What vehicles do we use?

How many different ways of travelling on land can you think of?

Make a list here.

Choose a vehicle and find out as much as you can about it. When was it invented? How many people can it carry? What makes it move? What else can you find out?

Write about it here.

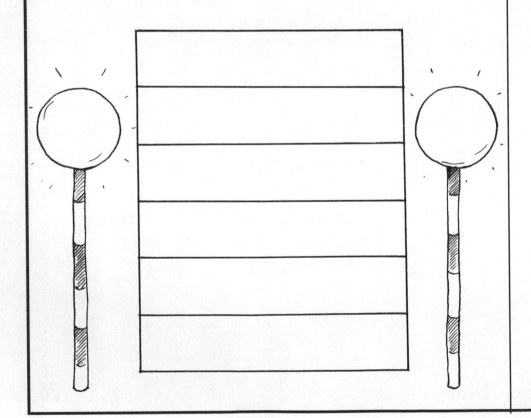

Writing

Off to work

Lots of people work in the world of transport.

♣ Choose a job that interests you. Here are some ideas.

pilot	taxi driver
flight attendant	train driver
sailor	bus driver
ship's captain	lorry driver

♣ Find out as much as you can about the job you have chosen. Use books and if you can talk to people who do the job.

♣ Write about the job using the World of work sheet.

Time for a story

Make up a short story that the younger children in your school may like.

♣ Choose one of these titles, or think of your own.

• Rover's Boat Adventure

• Helicopter Rescue!

• Up, Up and Away!

• The Terrific Train Trip

♣ Use the story strip sheet. Draw pictures and write short sentences about the six main points of the story.

Name _____

Find me!

Find me!

♣ Can you find twelve words in this puzzle? They are all types of transport. They read across, downwards and diagonally.

♣ Make a list of them. Time yourself and see how long it takes you to find them.

a	h	y	d	r	o	f	o	i	l	b	h
h	w	c	j	t	r	u	c	k	n	c	g
e	b	i	c	y	c	l	e	q	a	f	l
l	g	t	s	h	r	i	j	o	k	p	i
i	s	a	l	u	m	t	c	k	u	a	d
c	v	n	w	o	r	p	c	a	n	o	e
o	q	d	r	n	s	f	y	t	x	u	r
p	v	e	w	b	r	x	b	c	y	d	z
t	a	m	b	t	c	z	d	o	g	e	h
e	t	r	i	c	y	c	l	e	a	i	f
r	g	j	h	f	i	k	f	e	r	r	y
e	h	o	v	e	r	c	r	a	f	t	d

I can find these words:

1

2

3

4

5

6

7

8

9

10

11

12

It took me _____ minutes

Give us a clue!

Here is a finished crossword – except that the clues are missing!
♣ Write a clue for each answer. Clue number 1 across is already done.

		¹t	a	n	d	e	²m	
³c	a	r					o	
		a		⁴f			t	
⁵g	l	i	d	e	r		o	
		n		r			r	
	⁶c			r			b	
⁷l	o	r	r	y			i	
	a				⁸s	k	i
	⁹c	a	n	o	e		e	
	h						

Across

1 A bicycle made for two!

3

5

7

8

9

Down

1

2

4

6

Name _____

Sun time

Everyone is on the beach in the sunshine.

✤ Write about the picture. Here are some words to help you:
sunbathing
sun-cream
ice-cream
sand-castle
swimming
paddling

✤ Think of a title for your writing.

_____

_____

_____

_____

Writing

Heat wave

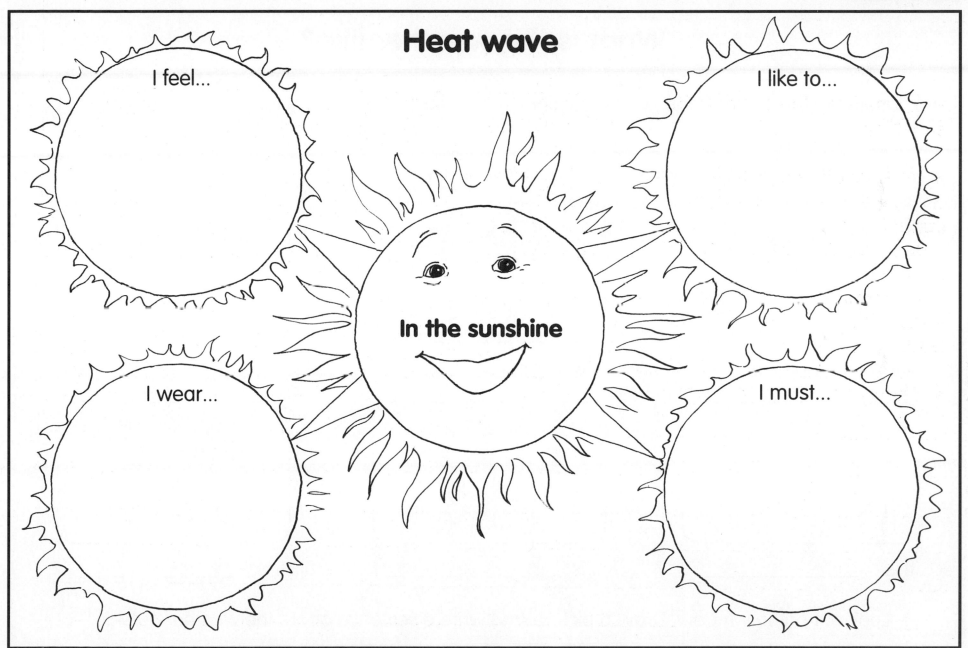

I feel...

I like to...

In the sunshine

I wear...

I must...

Name _____

What is the weather like?

What is the weather like?

| sunny | snowing | raining | foggy | windy | cloudy |

✤ Read the words above. Write them under the pictures to finish the sentences.

It is _____ .

It is _____ .

It is _____ .

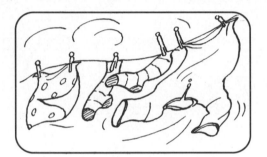

It is _____ .

It is _____ .

It is _____ .

✤ Look out of the window. Draw a picture and write a sentence about the weather outside.

Name _____

How do they feel?

How do the children feel? Why?

_____

_____

_____

_____

How does the girl feel? Why?

_____

_____

_____

_____

How does the farmer feel? Why?

_____

_____

_____

_____

How does the driver feel? Why?

_____

_____

_____

_____

Writing

Name _____

Holiday postcard

Holiday postcard

✤ Pretend you are on holiday, playing on a sunny beach.

✤ Write a postcard to your teacher and friends, with a short message. Write neatly and clearly.

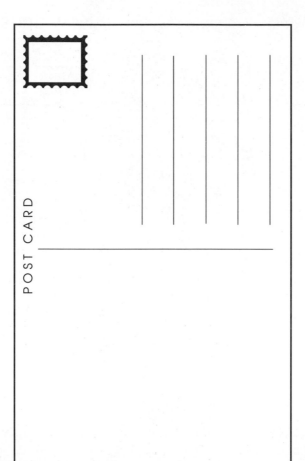

POST CARD

✤ Draw a picture for the front of your postcard. Show the beach where you are on holiday.

✤ Make up a name for the place and write it in the space at the top of your picture.

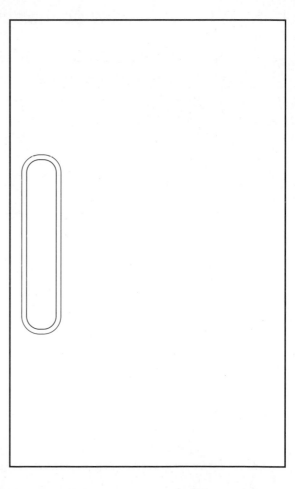

Writing

The weather is...

♣ Look at the pictures. What is the weather like?

♣ Follow the arrows and write down in the puzzle the word that finishes the sentence for that picture.

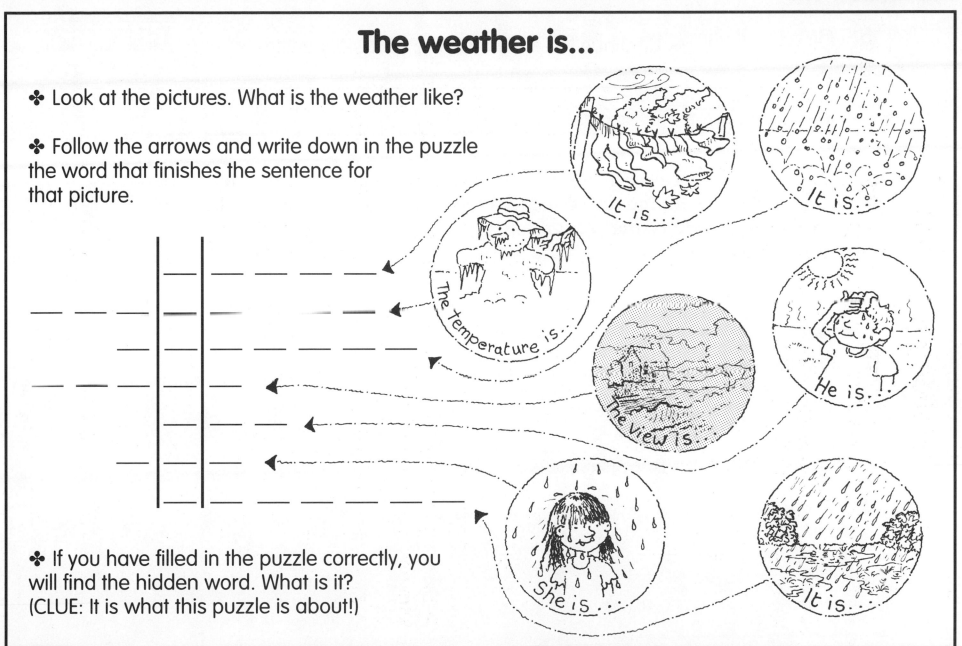

♣ If you have filled in the puzzle correctly, you will find the hidden word. What is it?
(CLUE: It is what this puzzle is about!)

Story start

Name _____

 ♣ Continue the story and give your story a title.

Caroline and her classmates stared out of the window in disbelief. Today was their class outing and outside the fog was so thick they couldn't see to the other side of the playground.

'Don't look so miserable,' said Mr Troy, their teacher. 'It's bound to clear soon. Let's get on the coach.'

Story middle

❖ Write a story with a beginning, a middle and an end. Use the sentences below as part of the **middle** of your story.

Gary suddenly woke up. He nudged James, who was in the sleeping bag next to him.
 'Was that thunder? It was very loud!'
 The rain was beating down on the tent. Soon, all the boys were awake. Gary looked at his watch. It was 2.20 am.

! Remember to give your story a title.

Story end

❖ Write a story with a beginning, a middle and an end. Use the sentences below as the **end** of your story.

'That certainly was a gale!' said Uncle Roger. 'Tomorrow, you children can clear away all the twigs and branches while I saw up this tree trunk. We can consider ourselves really lucky that it did not fall on the house!'

! Remember to give your story a title.

Faulty forecast

Weather forecasters don't always get it right!

✿ Imagine that you had planned a day out based on the weather forecast. However, the forecast was wrong. What happened?

✿ Write a letter of complaint to the weather forecaster. Tell him or her what you had planned, how the wrong forecast affected your plans and what happened in the end. Your letter can be funny, but remember to be polite!

TV weather person

Do you watch the weather news on TV? Who is your favourite weather presenter?

✿ Find out as much as you can about the job of a television weather presenter. (You could write a letter to your favourite weather person!)

✿ Write about the job of a television weather presenter using the World of work sheet.

Things you may want to know:
• What does the training involve?
• Does a weather presenter need to be able to forecast the weather?
• What hours does a weather presenter work?
• Does a weather presenter need to wear special clothes?
• Who helps the weather presenter do his or her job?
• How do the weather maps work?

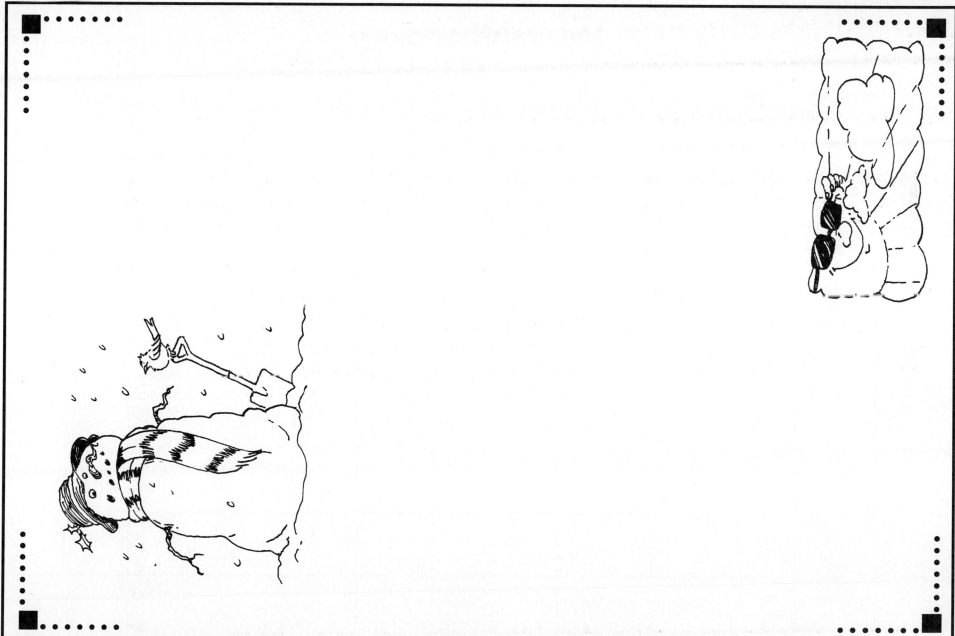

My weather diary

My weather diary

✤ Keep a weather diary for five school days. Write down the temperature each morning and afternoon. Write about the weather and draw a symbol each morning and afternoon. Here are some symbols you could use, or you could design your own.

	sunny	snowing	raining	foggy	windy	cloudy

Date	°C	Morning	Symbol	°C	Afternoon	Symbol

Writing

Bad weather!

❖ Read this poem.

Sounds of thunder!
Torrential rain!
Over the hills
Roll the clouds
Must be March again!

The first letter in each line can be read downwards to spell STORM – which Is what the poem is about!

❖ Try writing your own 'bad weather' poems about thunder and drought.

T _____
H _____
U _____
N _____
D _____
E _____
R _____

D _____
R _____
O _____
U _____
G _____
H _____
T _____

Drought

A drought happens when the weather is very hot and dry for a long time and there is no rain.
A drought causes many difficulties. Can you say what they are? Here are some clues:

water   **plants**   **animals**   **birds**   **hosepipes**   **fires**

Write about problems caused by drought. How are they solved? How can we help to prevent them?

Snow

❖ Read these sentences:

As I came out of the **gloomy** house, I blinked at the **dazzling** light reflected from the **bright**, **white** snow, which lay on the ground like a **huge** blanket. The **once-sharp** edges and corners of roofs and chimneys above me were now gently **rounded** and **curved** by the **soft**, **new** snow.

The sentences describe what someone saw when it had been snowing.

❖ Write your own snowy story using adjectives. (Adjectives are describing words such as those in bold in the passage above.)

Name _____

Newsworthy

♣ What has happened? Write a report for your local newspaper.
♣ Give your report an eye-catching headline.
♣ Write a caption for the picture.

Weekly News

Animal farm

What a lot of animals!

♣ Write about the picture.
Here are some words to help you:

duck	rabbits
llama	geese
donkey	chickens
owl	kittens
pony	dragonflies
tortoise	pond

♣ Think of a title for your writing.

_____

_____

_____

_____

_____

_____

Name _____

How do they move?

❖ How do these animals move?

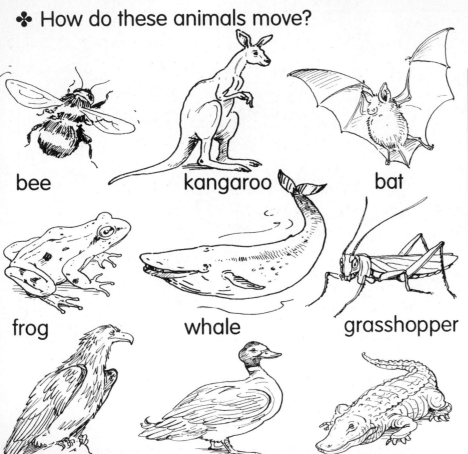

bee

kangaroo

bat

frog

whale

grasshopper

eagle

duck

alligator

❖ Fill in the chart.
❖ Write down two more animals for each column.

Animals that swim	Animals that fly	Animals that jump

❖ If you could choose, how would you like to be able to move? _____

❖ On the back of this sheet, draw a picture of yourself moving in this way.

Caring for a pet

❖ Think of a pet you would like to look after. You might choose one of these:

cat	dog	hamster
gerbil	fish	budgerigar
guinea pig	rabbit	pony

❖ What important things would you need to remember while caring for this pet?
Think about:

food	drink	sleeping and
grooming	exercise	living quarters

❖ Write about, and draw a picture of, each step in your care programme using the story strip sheet.

A puppy is for life!

You want to buy a puppy. The owner, Mr Norbutt, has asked you to write him a letter saying why you would be a suitable person to give the dog a good home.

❖ Think carefully about what you will write. Consider:

• your thoughts and feelings about the responsibility of having a pet
  • exercise
  • food
  • drink
  • grooming
  • sleeping quarters

❖ Use the letter template under your writing paper.

Letter-writing paper

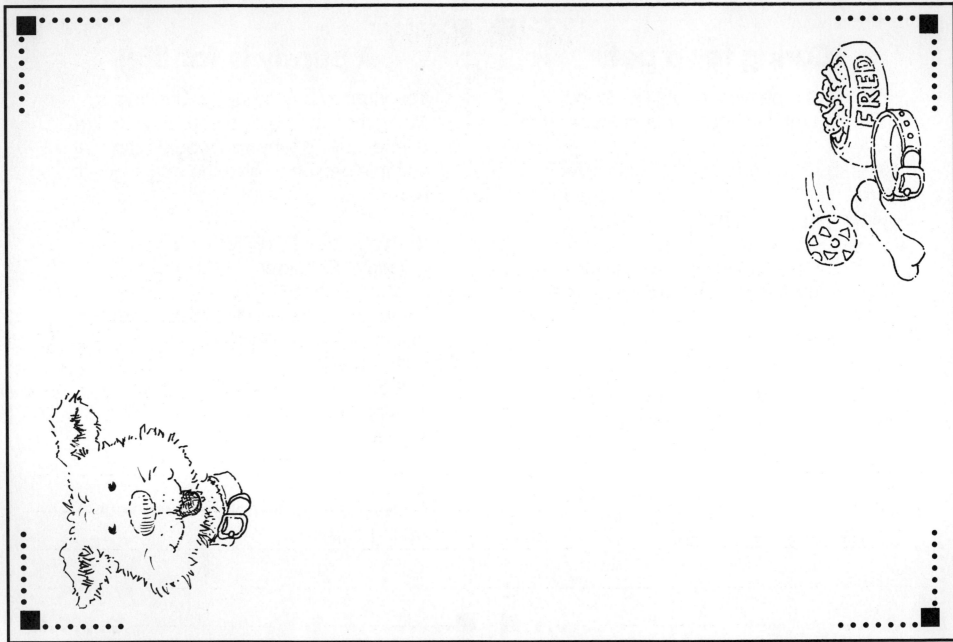

Name _____

Mr Pricklepin

_____

_____

_____

_____

_____

Name _____

Freddie the fish

Freddie the fish

_____

_____

_____

_____

_____

Name _____

Leo the lion

Name _____

Read all about it

♣ Write a newspaper article to go with this headline and draw a picture to go with it.

♣ Remember to give your picture a caption.

Zoo News Gazette   ◆ **Wednesday** 23 October

Efforts fail to save zoo from closure

Name _____

Where is it?

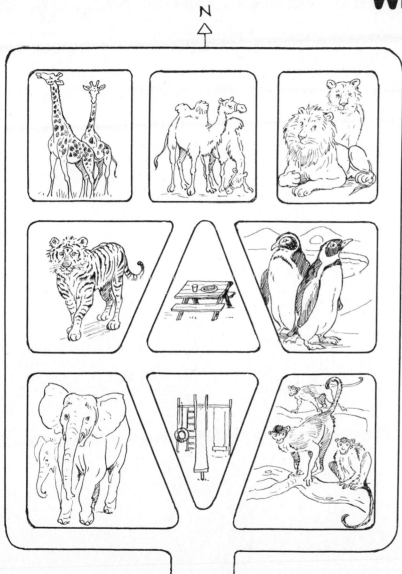

♣ Write about the map. Fill in the gaps below by choosing from the following words:

| north | south | east | west |

The restaurant is _____ of the camels.

The giraffes are _____ of the camels.

The lions are _____ of the penguins.

The elephants are _____ of the tigers.

The monkeys are _____ of the play area.

The restaurant is _____ of the play area.

♣ Now fill in these gaps.

The _____ is west of the penguins.

The _____ are south of the giraffes.

The _____ is east of the elephants.

The _____ are north of the _____ .

Story start

 ♣ Continue the story and give your story a title.

Once upon a time, long, long ago, there was a weird and wonderful forest. In this weird and wonderful forest were some amazing, magical creatures.

Story middle

❖ Write a story with a beginning, a middle and an end. Use the sentences below as part of the **middle** of your story.

Just at the edge of the field, where some people had had a picnic, we saw it – a poor little baby rabbit with badly cut paws. Broken bottles and opened cans were scattered around.

❗ Remember to give your story a title.

Story end

❖ Write a story with a beginning, a middle and an end. Use the sentences below as the **end** of your story.

Everyone in the school felt so proud! We had saved all these beautiful plants from being churned up by the digger which was making the new road. Some of the plants were quite rare, but now there was a chance that they would multiply and new seedlings would grow.

❗ Remember to give your story a title.

Name _____

Safari park poster

Safari park poster

♣ Design an exciting poster to advertise a special day at the safari park – perhaps a 'Family Picnic Day' or a 'Safari I-Spy Tour'.

♣ Inform the public of the type of event, date, place, time, cost, attractions and so on.

♣ Make the poster clear and colourful.

Writing

Let's talk!

Write your conversation here.

♣ Here are some simple handmade puppets. Write a conversation between two puppets. It could be between two of these puppets or two of your own.

♣ Make your puppets and use them to act out the conversation to the other children in your class.

Name _____

My farm-i-o!

My farm-i-o!

Chorus:
There are dogs and cats and fleas and flies,
And they all live on my farm-i-o.
Elephants, ants, hippopotami too;
Everyone thinks I'm barmy-o!

Verse 1

I love my dogs. I love my cats.
I even love my vampire bats.
I've horses too, and
Butterflies blue,
And they all live on my farm-i-o.

♣ These are the chorus and first verse of a very silly song! Make up verses 2 and 3. Do a rough draft first. Then, when you are happy with it, neatly copy out the words here.

Verse 2

Verse 3

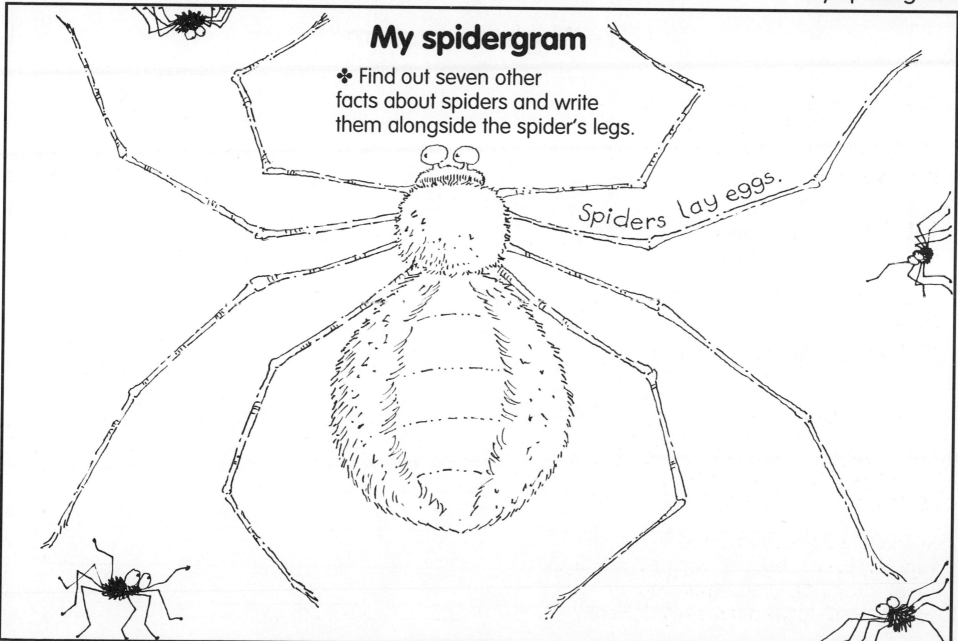

My spidergram

♣ Find out seven other
facts about spiders and write
them alongside the spider's legs.

Spiders lay eggs.

Let's go for a swim

Name _____

Let's go for a swim

Everyone is having fun.

♣ Write about the picture. Here are some words to help you:

water	fountain
pool	armbands
tube	paddling
slide	swimming
floats	diving

♣ Think of a title for your writing.

_____

_____

_____

_____

_____

_____

Writing

Waterfall crossword

❖ Write the name of each picture in the squares. Number one has already been done for you.

Label it

Name _____

Label it

♣ Put the right labels on the goods in the shop window.

WET WEAR

| towel | boots | swimming-costume | goggles | mac | armbands | umbrella | trunks | hat |

Writing

Wet! Wet! Wet!

♣ Write a caption for each picture.

 paddling

 diving

 jumping

_____

_____

 watering

 swimming

 drinking

_____

_____

Writing

89

Name _____

Finish and join

All the objects below can hold water.
♣ Finish the words and join them up to the right pictures.

b _ _ l

c _ _

b _ _ _ le

t _ _

j _ _

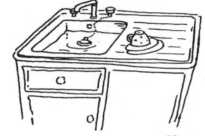

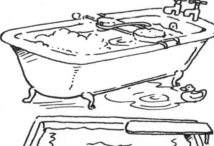

sw _ m _ _ _ g

p _ _ l

b _ _ _

p _ d _ l _ _ g

p _ _ l

s _ n _

Writing

Name _____

At the seaside

I see

I smell

I feel

I like

All jumbled up!

All jumbled up!

♣ Read these sentences.

I dry my face and hands.
Then I turn on the taps.
After I have washed, I comb my hair.
I put the plug in.
Lastly, I clean my teeth.
Then I wash my face.
I take out the plug.
First, I wash my hands.

They are in the wrong order.

♣ Write them out again on the right-hand side of this page in the right order.
♣ At the end, write down some things that you might do next.

It sounds like rain!

♣ Read this rainy poem.

Drip.
Drop.
Drip. Drop.
Drip. Drop.
Pitter. Patter.
Pitter. Patter.
Patter.
Splash!
Patter.
Splash!
Splish. Splash.
Splish. Splash.
CRASH!
FLASH!

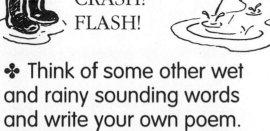

♣ Think of some other wet and rainy sounding words and write your own poem. You could use some of the words in this poem as well.

♣ Write your poem here. Draw a picture to go with your poem.

Name _____

Frogs

❖ Find a book that will tell you about frogs. Look at the pictures below.
❖ Write a sentence about each picture, using the words to help you.

eggs **frogspawn**

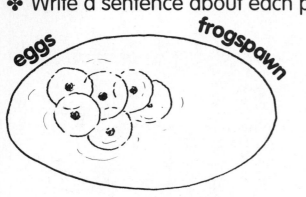

tadpoles

legs **frogs**

_____

_____

land **freshwater**

water insects

❖ Draw your own picture of a frog here.

_____

_____

Name _____

Fresh water or salt water?

Below are the names of some creatures that live in fresh water or salt water.

✤ Find out which creatures live where.
✤ Choose one colour for freshwater animals and another for salt-water animals. Colour them in.

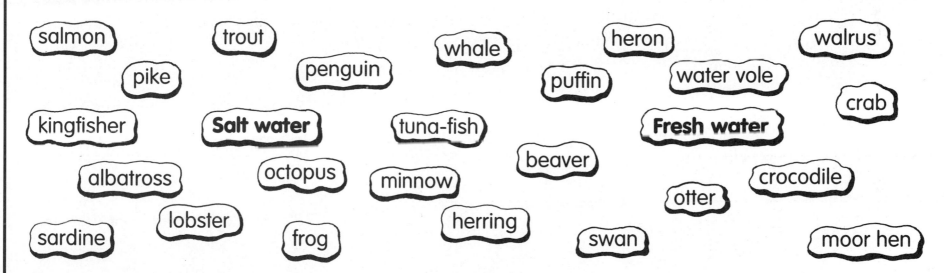

salmon trout whale heron walrus

pike penguin puffin water vole

kingfisher **Salt water** tuna-fish **Fresh water** crab

octopus beaver

albatross minnow crocodile

otter

lobster herring moor hen

sardine frog swan

✤ Choose one creature that interests you and find out about it. Write about it here.

_____

_____

_____

_____

Story start

Name _____

 ♣ Continue the story and give your story a title.

Satnam and Nida were so excited. They had never been on a river boat before. As they climbed on board with their parents, they saw a large sign: LIFE-JACKETS MUST BE WORN AT ALL TIMES.

Story middle

♣ Write a story with a beginning, a middle and an end. Use the sentences below as part of the **middle** of your story.

I looked at our raft with pride. We had made it from two large barrels and a plank of wood. There was no doubt that we would win the race. I handed the paddles to Jim and Sophie.

'Ready! Steady! Go!' shouted the starter.

! Remember to give your story a title.

Story end

♣ Write a story with a beginning, a middle and an end. Use the sentences below as the **end** of your story.

Despite that one mishap, everyone had enjoyed the afternoon at the pond, and we were glad we had taken all our pond-dipping things with us. We had seen whirligig beetles, water-boatmen, pond skaters, a dragonfly and lots of other pond creatures.

! Remember to give your story a title.

Water Weekly   ✦ **Wednesday** 23 October

The crazy boat race

The headline for this photograph suggests the event was great fun.

♣ Write an article about the picture.

Here are some ideas to help you:

- How many teams?
- Team names?
- What sort of boats?
- How far to race?
- What happened during the race?
- Which team won?

♣ Write a caption for the picture.

The water cycle

The water cycle is the story of how rain is made. It starts from the sea and finishes in the sea.

✤ Using the story strip sheet, draw pictures and write sentences to describe the water cycle. You may need to do some research.

Here are some words to help you:

evaporates
air currents
cloud over land
rain and snow
streams and rivers
the sea
water vapour

The life-guard

At most swimming pools you will see life-guards patrolling the pool. They are there to make sure that everyone is safe in the water.

✤ Write a letter to the life-guard at your local swimming pool, asking him or her about the job. Use the letter template under your writing paper.

Find out this information:
• Why did they choose the job?
• How and where did they train for it?
• What are their duties?
• What is their uniform?
• What problems do they have to sort out in the pool?
• What hours do they work?

Letter-writing paper

Name _____

It's party time!

It is someone's birthday.

♣ Write about the picture.

Here are some words to help you:

cake	sausages
biscuits	jug
crisps	candles
balloons	hats
party poppers	sandwiches

♣ Think of a title for your writing.

_____

_____

_____

_____

_____

Name _____

Choose the colour

Choose the colour

✤ Join the foods to the right colour.
✤ Write a sentence about each food. The first one has been done for you.

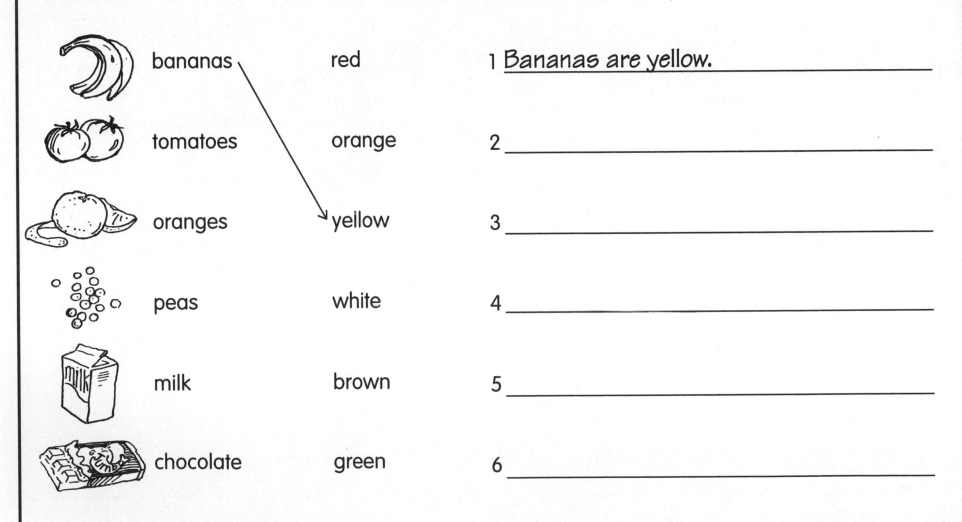

bananas	red	1 <u>Bananas are yellow.</u>
tomatoes	orange	2 _____
oranges	yellow	3 _____
peas	white	4 _____
milk	brown	5 _____
chocolate	green	6 _____

Writing

What should we eat?

♣ Add some more foods to the lists below. The pictures will give you some ideas.

♣ Can you think of any others?

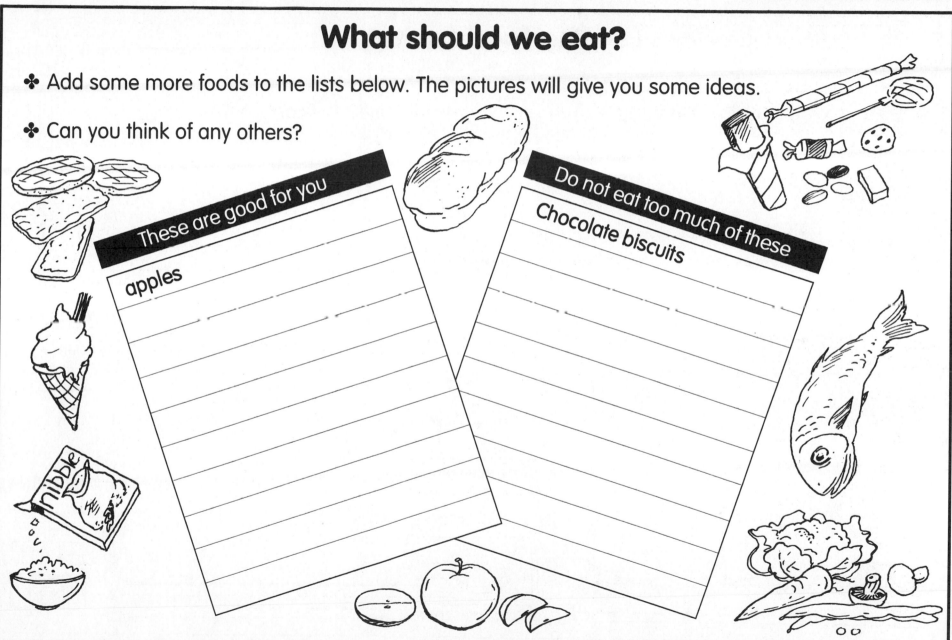

These are good for you

apples

Do not eat too much of these

Chocolate biscuits

Name _____

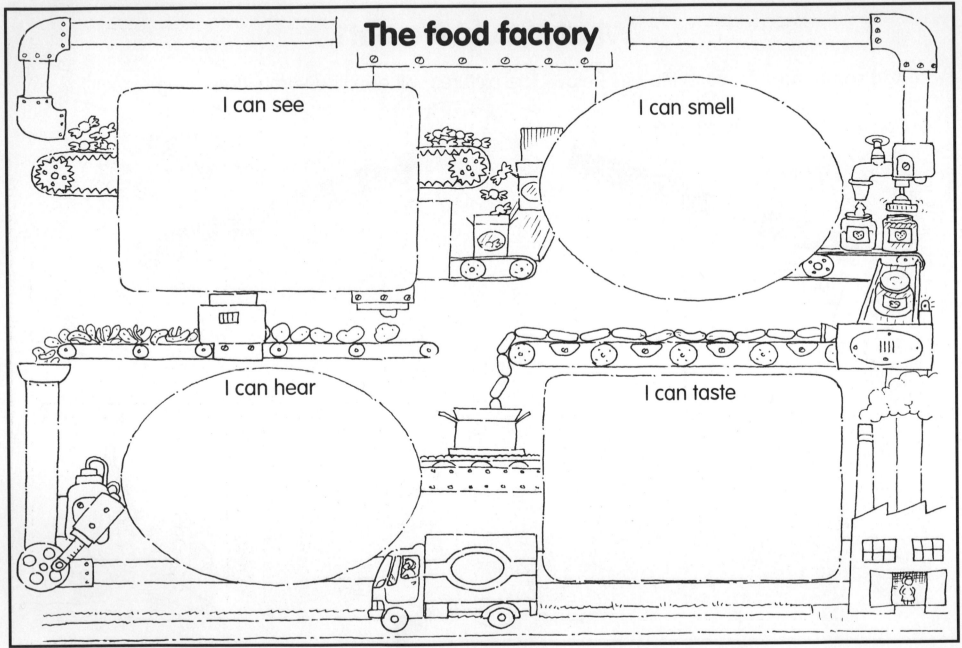

The food factory

I can see

I can smell

I can hear

I can taste

Writing

What happened?

♣ Tell the story.

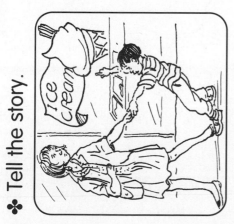

♣ What happened next?

Name _____

Healthy eating

Eating good food keeps you healthy and strong.

✤ What are the healthy foods in the pictures? Write their names in the puzzle.
Some letters have been put in to help you.

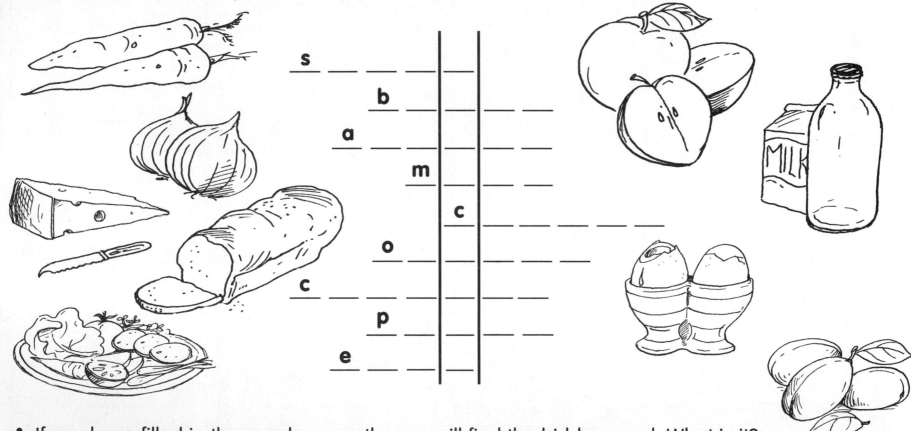

s _ _ _ _

b _ _ _ _

a _ _ _ _ _

m _ _ _

c _ _ _ _ _ _

o _ _ _ _

c _ _ _ _ _

p _ _ _ _

e _ _ _ _

✤ If you have filled in the puzzle correctly, you will find the hidden word. What is it?
(CLUE: It is what all these foods are!)

Writing

Let's go shopping

❖ Look at the pictures. Write a shopping list in alphabetical order.

a b c d e f g h i j k l m n o p q r s t u v w x y z

❖ Think of food items for your shopping list which begin with the letters of the alphabet not yet been used.

Story start

Name _____

 ❖ Continue the story and give your story a title.

Simon was happy. It was a beautiful day, just right for a picnic. He and his family had driven to the countryside and were looking for a suitable place to stop. Suddenly, the car went over a large bump in the road and everyone giggled.

'I hope you packed that picnic basket in the back tightly,' said Simon's dad to his mum.

'Me?' she said. 'I thought *you* put it in the car!'

Story middle

❖ Write a story with a beginning, a middle and an end. Use the sentences below as part of the **middle** of your story.

All of a sudden Naomi smelled something burning. She raced back into the kitchen, grabbed the oven gloves and opened the oven door. What she saw was not a pretty sight.

! Remember to give your story a title.

Story end

❖ Write a story with a beginning, a middle and an end. Use the sentences below as the **end** of your story.

Finally the judges stood up.
  'I am pleased to announce', said the spokesperson, 'that the winner of this year's pizza-eating competition – by one third of a pizza – is Sammy Sampson'.
  As the cheers went up, all Sammy could do was grin weakly. He felt far too full to do anything else.

! Remember to give your story a title.

Who's cooking?

Who cooks the lunch in your school? It may be the cook with some helpers.

✣ Find out as much as you can about the cook's job. You may be able to interview him or her.

✣ Use the World of work sheet and write about the school cook's job.

Some useful questions:
- What time do you start work?
- Where does the food come from?
- What is your favourite job?
- What is the job you like least?

Invent a lolly

An ice-cream company is holding a competition for new ideas for ice-lollies.

✣ Invent an exciting new kind of lolly.

✣ Write a letter to the company describing your invention. Use the letter template under your writing paper.

Don't forget to tell them about the **flavour, colour** and **shape** of your ice-lolly. You could suggest an advertising slogan to sell it. You will need to draw a coloured picture of your lolly.

Name _____

Let's have a party

Let's have a party

♣ Make your own party invitation.

♣ Design your invitation on some rough paper first, then draw the final version here.

What sort of party will it be?
- fancy dress
- barbecue
- video party
- birthday party
- Christmas party
- firework party

Where will the party be held?

On what date?

At what time will it start and finish?

♣ Include a reply slip.

♣ Decorate your invitation to show what type of party you are having.

RSVP

Let's have a barbecue

Barbecues are fun! Delicious food is cooked over charcoal in the open air.

♣ Choose a menu for a barbecue.

Choose food for:
• starters
• main courses
• desserts
• nibbles
• drinks

♣ Design the menu. Write clearly and illustrate it.

Name _____

The sandwich bar

The sandwich bar

What is your favourite type of sandwich?
♣ Write down the recipe for making your favourite sandwich.

Ingredients:

What to do:

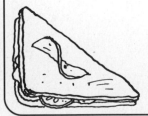

♣ Invent some different, exciting sandwich fillings. List six of them.

1

2

3

4

5

6

Writing

Tasty crossword

Here is a finished crossword.

♣ Write a clue for each answer. Number 1 across has been done for you.

Across

1 A hot dish from India.

4

6

8

9

12

14

15

16

Down

1

2

3

5

7

10

11

13

14

The completed crossword grid contains the following answers:

Across: 1 curry, 4 ham, 6 apple, 8 carrot, 9 sugar, 12 meat, 14 chips, 15 nuts, 16 raisin

Down: 1 chops, 2 roast, 3 cheese, 5 spaghetti, 7 pear, 10 gravy, 11 pasta, 13 tuna, 14 cone

Fire! Fire!

Fire! Fire!

The house is on fire!

♣ Write about the picture. Here are some words to help you:

house	hose
family	pets
budgerigar	ladder
fire-engine	fireman
smoke	flames
police car	policeman

♣ Think of a title for your writing.

_____

_____

_____

_____

_____

Dental wordsearch

There are lots of words hidden in this square to do with looking after our teeth.
They read across and downwards.

♣ Find the words and draw a ring round each one. The first has been done for you.

teeth ✓ **dentist**   **brush**   **paste** **smile**   **decay**   **germs**   **clean**   **X-rays**   **sugar**   **gums**

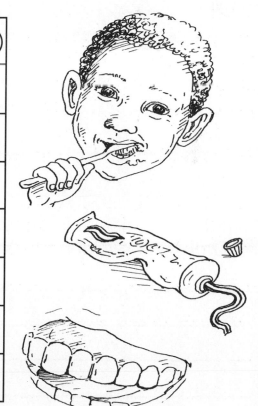

x	b	a	t	e	e	t	h
s	g	s	u	g	a	r	d
g	u	m	s	c	x	p	e
e	a	i	y	l	r	a	n
r	l	l	a	e	a	s	t
m	d	e	c	a	y	t	i
s	u	b	a	n	s	e	s
b	s	b	r	u	s	h	t

Spot the hazards!

Spot the hazards!

What in this picture is dangerous?
♣ Draw a ring around the hazards you can spot and write about them.

_____

_____

_____

_____

Out and about

♣ Think about six important safety rules to remember when you are near a road.

♣ Use the story strip sheet to write about each rule. Draw a picture for each one.

• Make your writing small and neat.

• Make your pictures simple and clear.

This is my job!

♣ Choose a person whose job it is to keep you healthy or safe.

Here is a list of some of them:

policewoman   lollipop person
life-guard   doctor
fireman   dentist

You may think of others.

♣ Find out as much as you can about the job you have chosen by using books and talking to people.

♣ Write about the job on your World of work sheet.

Name _____

Beware!

Beware!

Look at the pictures of things that can be dangerous.

♣ Can you find eight words in the square that match the eight pictures? They may be downwards or across. Draw a ring round each word. One has been done for you.

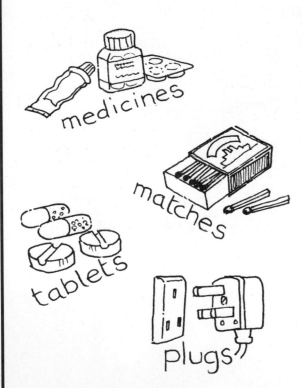

medicines

matches

tablets

plugs

a	m	y	b	z	c	a	d	x	e	y	f
g	e	l	e	c	t	r	i	c	i	t	y
b	d	h	c	i	d	j	e	k	f	l	g
m	i	n	q	t	o	h	p	i	q	e	r
r	c	s	m	a	t	c	h	e	s	t	i
u	i	v	k	b	l	w	m	x	n	y	v
z	n	a	o	l	b	p	f	i	r	e	e
c	e	d	q	e	r	f	s	g	o	h	r
i	s	j	u	t	k	v	l	w	a	m	s
n	x	o	y	s	q	z	r	a	d	t	b
u	c	v	d	w	p	l	u	g	s	x	e
b	d	h	c	i	d	j	e	k	f	l	g

electricity

rivers

fire

roads

Writing

Healthy food

If you want to be healthy, you have to eat the right sorts of food. This dinner plate here shows some of the different foods we can eat to give us the proteins, fats, carbohydrates, vitamins, minerals and fibre we need to stay healthy.

♣ Can you spot the foods that appear in more than one section?

♣ Choose one type of food from each section and draw these on your own dinner plate showing a healthy meal you would like to eat.

♣ Write a menu for your meal. What will you choose to drink?

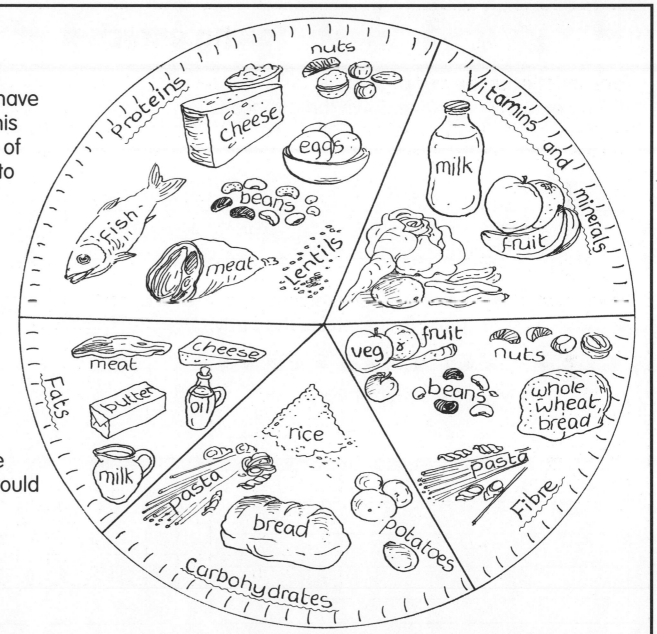

Name _____

Taking exercise!

Taking exercise!

Exercise is good for our bodies.
♣ Find out why and write down three reasons.

1 _____

2 _____

3 _____

Playing sport is a good way of exercising.
♣ Make a list of sports that exercise the body.

♣ Choose one of the sports and write about it.

My list of sports

_____

_____

_____

_____

✣ Continue the story and give your story a title.

Zahid was riding his new bike. He saw some of his friends coming down the street and he wanted to show off.

'Look,' he shouted. 'I can ride with no hands.'

As he rode off, his front wheel hit a stone and he felt the bike swerve.

Story middle

❖ Write a story with a beginning, a middle and an end. Use the sentences below as part of the **middle** of your story.

Without thinking, Richard ran after it, straight into the road. There was a loud squeal of brakes from a car.

❗ Remember to give your story a title.

Story end

❖ Write a story with a beginning, a middle and an end. Use the sentences below as the **end** of your story.

The noise grew louder and I realised with relief that the rescue helicopter was near. I was soon winched to safety and taken to the hospital for a check-up. Although the worst of it was now over, I knew it wasn't going to be easy explaining things to my parents.

❗ Remember to give your story a title.

Competition time!

A competition is being run to design a road safety poster for very young children.

✤ Can you design a winning poster? It must remind the children to be careful when they are near the road.
These words must be on your poster:

STOP !   LOOK !   LISTEN !   WALK !

Will you use any other words?

Name _____

Toothy tales

❖ Read these questions.

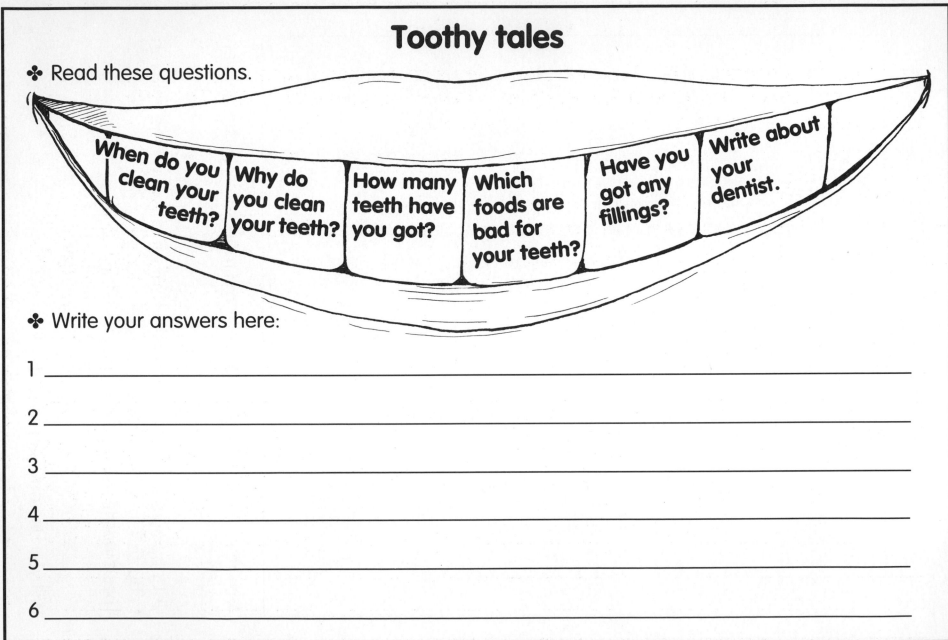

When do you clean your teeth?

Why do you clean your teeth?

How many teeth have you got?

Which foods are bad for your teeth?

Have you got any fillings?

Write about your dentist.

❖ Write your answers here:

1 _____

2 _____

3 _____

4 _____

5 _____

6 _____

Water safety

Water can be dangerous, even if you can swim. The pictures below show some of the accidents that can occur in or near the water.

✤ Write a sentence for each picture, describing how to avoid the danger. The first has been done for you.

When you are in a boat,
sit still and don't lean out.

Safety rhymes

Sometimes a silly rhyme can help you to remember something important.

✤ Adapt a nursery rhyme and write a verse which reminds people about road safety.

Here is one to start you off, based on 'I hear thunder/Frère Jacques'.

> I hear traffic, I hear traffic,
> Rushing past, rushing past,
> Wait until the road's clear,
> Wait until the road's clear,
> Safe at last! Safe at last!

My rhyme

On the road

Road signs are important. You can find out what they all mean by looking in The Highway Code.

 Circular signs give orders

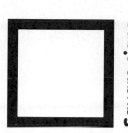 Triangular signs give warnings

Square signs give information

✿ Find out what these signs mean. Write the meaning underneath the sign.

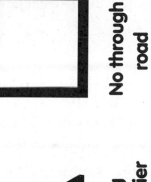 Hospital

✿ Find out what these signs should look like. Complete the signs.

No pedestrians

Level crossing ahead with barrier or gate

No through road

Name _____

Keep fit!

Keep fit!

❖ Can you find 12 words in this wordsearch? All are things which help us to keep fit and healthy.

❖ Time yourself and see how long it takes you to find the words.
They read downwards, across and diagonally.

❖ Make a list of the words:

l	s	m	t	n	u	o	v	p	w	q	x	r
a	t	o	o	t	h	b	r	u	s	h	v	b
v	c	n	u	r	s	e	d	v	e	s	i	f
e	g	w	o	d	e	n	t	i	s	t	t	h
g	i	x	j	u	y	k	z	e	l	w	a	m
e	n	a	o	b	r	p	n	q	c	a	m	r
t	e	x	e	r	c	i	s	e	s	r	i	t
a	u	d	v	e	l	d	s	w	f	m	n	x
b	y	w	g	n	z	o	a	h	b	t	s	p
l	c	h	a	d	j	c	k	e	m	h	e	g
e	h	e	f	t	i	t	j	l	k	e	l	m
s	l	m	a	n	e	o	b	p	l	q	n	c
c	r	d	s	e	t	r	f	s	g	u	h	t

It took me _____ minutes to complete the wordsearch.

Letter template

Address

Date

Salutation

Letter

Closing

Sender's name

Envelope template

✤ Follow these instructions to make your envelope:

- Cut along the outside lines.

- Fold flaps 1 and 2 inwards along the dotted lines.

- Fold flap 3 upwards along the dotted line.

- Glue flap 3 to flaps 1 and 2.

- Insert your letter.

- Fold flap 4 downwards along the dotted line.

- Glue flap 4 down to seal the envelope.

Remember to address your envelope correctly.

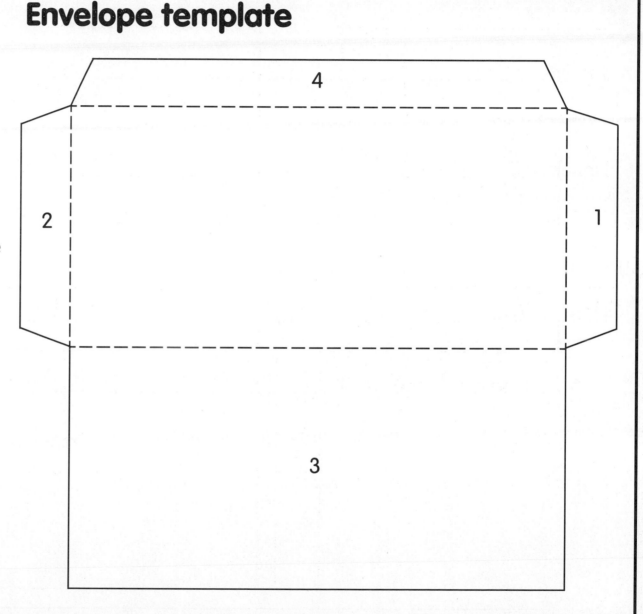

Name _____

World of work sheet

World of work

Job title _____

Place of work _____

Uniform _____

Duties _____

Equipment used _____

Hours of work _____

A working day in the life of _____

Title: _____

Author: _____

Publisher: _____

Hardback or paperback? _____

Price: _____

Critic: _____

Characters:

Setting:

Time:

Story line:

Best bits!

Recommended for:

☆ rating (tick box)

☆ | ☆☆ | ☆☆☆

My diary

Name _____

Month: _____   **Year:** _____

○ *Monday*   ○ *Thursday*

○ *Tuesday*   ○ *Friday*

○ *Wednesday*   ○ *Saturday*

                              ○ *Sunday*

The great debate

❖ **What is the issue?**

❖ **Consider the arguments:**

FOR	AGAINST

Name _____

Book jacket

✤ Design a book jacket for a story or book that you have written or read.
Look at different book jackets to find out what information to include.

Back cover   Spine   Front cover

Writing

Sell it!

❖ Write a radio advertisement to sell this new product:

❖ Think of a catchy jingle or slogan that is easy to remember.

Punctuation

✿ Put in the missing capital letters and full stops.

on monday mrs evans did her washing she washed her skirt

and jumper it was not raining so she hung them up to dry in

the garden then she went to the shops to buy some food for

her dinner when she got back home she looked in the garden

all her washing was gone

✿ Put in the missing punctuation.

when you look at a turtle what do you see you see an animal

that looks like a tortoise you might think to yourself there is no

difference but you would be wrong for you may see a turtle

swimming in water but you will never see a tortoise swimming

in water

✿ Put in the missing punctuation.

ben and jane were very excited they had been invited to a

christmas party oh what shall i wear said jane shall i wear my

best jeans and jumper perhaps i should wear my blue dress

what will you wear to the party ben she asked i am going to

wear my spaceman suit said ben

Alphabet Arthur

A C E G I
B D F H J K
L M
N
z y x
w v u t s r q p o n O
m P
l
k
j
i
h
f g
a b c d e Q
R
Z
T S
X V
Y W U

✤ Finish drawing Alphabet Arthur by joining up the dots in the right order. First join the capital letters and then join the small letters. Don't mix them up!

✤ Write about Arthur.

Name _____

What's the message?

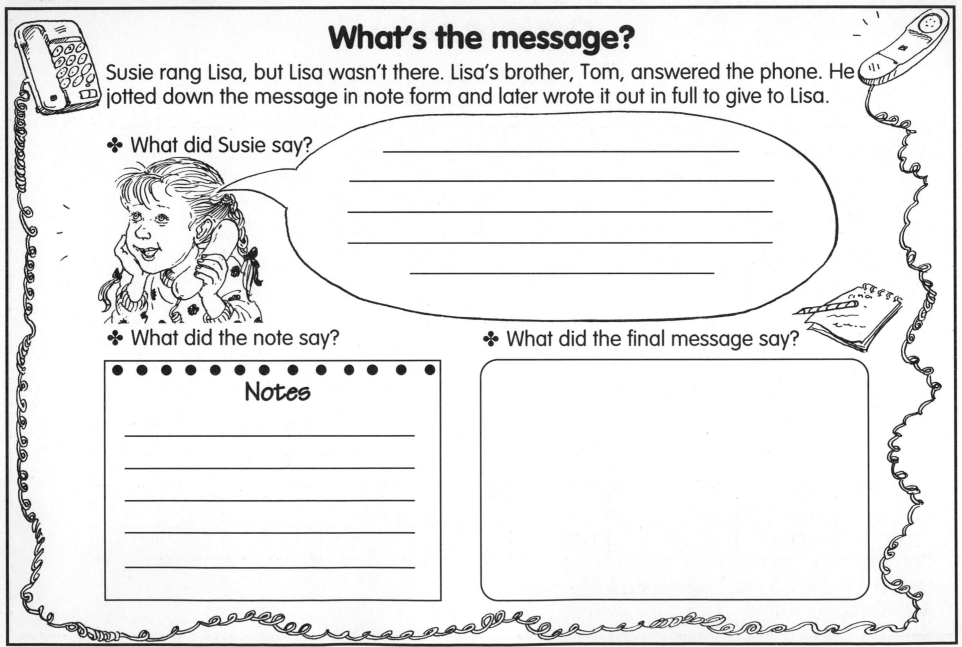

What's the message?

Susie rang Lisa, but Lisa wasn't there. Lisa's brother, Tom, answered the phone. He jotted down the message in note form and later wrote it out in full to give to Lisa.

❖ What did Susie say?

_____

_____

_____

_____

_____

❖ What did the note say?

Notes

_____

_____

_____

_____

❖ What did the final message say?

Crack the code!

A	B	C	D	E	F	G	H	I	J	K	L	M	N	O	P	Q	R	S	T	U	V	W	X	Y	Z
1	2	3	4	5	6	7	8	9	10	11	12	13	14	15	16	17	18	19	20	21	22	23	24	25	26

Each letter has a number.

♣ Work out the following message. Write the letters in the boxes.

3	1	14		25	15	21		3	15	13	5		20	15		20	5	1		15	14

13	15	14	4	1	25	**?**

♣ Now make up your own message in code.

♣ Give the message to your friend to decode.

Name _____

Picture puzzle

Picture puzzle

♣ What does this say? Each picture makes a word or part of a word. Work out the message and write it down here.

♣ Make up some picture writing of your own.